M000200140

"The publication of Iman Mersal's *The Threshold* is a major literary event. Long recognized throughout the Arab world and in Europe, Mersal is one of the strongest confessional (or postconfessional) poets we now have, in any language: her poems are fueled by a mordant wit, sensual vibrancy, and feminist brio. Impatient with pieties—whether political, erotic, or poetic—she writes, like Louise Glück, with emotional intensity and analytic coolness. This is poetry of earned and perfect pitch: the notations of an impassioned mind."
—MAUREEN N. McLANE, author of *More Anon*

"Mersal's poems are many things—sensuous, cerebral, intimate, angry and disorientating. They provide food for thought and elicit laughter in the dark . . . [*The Threshold* is] a perfect entry point for readers new to her work." **—MALCOLM FORBES**, *The National*

"Mersal's work is unafraid of its own promontories and edges . . . Many of the poems read like missives of faith addressed to a shadowy, mirrored world of choices unmade and lives unlived, now assuming the force of a haunting." **—ALEX TAN**, *Asymptote*

"Undeceived, ironic, daring, Iman Mersal's poems are animated by a singular sensibility. They deal candidly with real life—migration, dying parents, emotional entanglements—and discover general truths among the fine particulars. Robyn Creswell's translation is deft and subtle, and the Anglophone world is lucky to have it." **—NICK LAIRD**, author of *Feel Free*

"In a voice both fluid and laser-focused, fierce and tenuous, unflinching and vulnerable, [Iman Mersal] hews a path that is post-Arab-modernist, unsettling certainties about the ground from which an individual sees and speaks." **—ELIZABETH T. GRAY JR.**, *Book Post*

THE

THRESHOLD

FARRAR STRAUS GIROUX

NEW YORK

THE

THRESHOLD

IMAN MERSAL

TRANSLATED FROM THE ARABIC BY

ROBYN CRESWELL

Farrar, Straus and Giroux
120 Broadway, New York 10271

Published in 2022 by Farrar, Straus and Giroux
First paperback edition, 2023

The Library of Congress has cataloged the hardcover edition as follows:
Names: Mirsāl, Īmān, author. | Creswell, Robyn, translator.
Title: The threshold : poems / Iman Mersal ; translated from the Arabic by
Robyn Creswell.
Other titles: Threshold (Compilation)
Description: First edition. | New York : Farrar, Straus and Giroux, 2022.
Identifiers: LCCN 2022022689 | ISBN 9780374604271 (hardcover)
Subjects: LCSH: Mirsāl, Īmān—Translations into English. | LCGFT: Poetry.
Classification: LCC PJ7846.I64 T48 2022 | DDC 892.7/16—dc23/eng20220513
LC record available at https://lccn.loc.gov/2022022689

Paperback ISBN: 978-0-374-60785-2

Designed by Crisis

Our books may be purchased in bulk for promotional, educational, or
business use. Please contact your local bookseller or the Macmillan
Corporate and Premium Sales Department at 1-800-221-7945, extension
5442, or by email at MacmillanSpecialMarkets@macmillan.com.

www.fsgbooks.com
www.twitter.com/fsgbooks
www.facebook.com/fsgbooks

CONTENTS

"Where are all the wasted days?" asks Iman Mersal in a poem called "CV." Running her eyes down the official version of her life, "scrubbed free of dirt," the poet wonders where the black depressions and empty hours have gone, all the experiments that ended in failure. "There isn't a single open window," she frets, looking at the sheer list of accomplishments, "and no trace of the desire, deferred, to leap out." Mersal's poems acknowledge many fantasies of escape, including the self-destructive kind, and she knows that the persona we present to the world is often just a useful alibi. ("I'm pretty sure / my self-exposures / are for me to hide behind," as she wryly puts it.) The CV is a fantasy of a different order: not a leap into the unknown, but a self-satisfied retrospect; not a persona, but the negation of personhood. In other words, it's a tombstone disguised as a hot-air balloon. "Proof," as Mersal writes, "that the one who lived it / has cut all ties to the earth." Is there a way to write one's life that remains tied to the ground? Can one make poetry of even the seemingly wasted days?

To grasp the power and originality of Mersal's art, it's helpful to know something about the recent past of Arabic poetry. The canon of Arabic verse from the 1950s through the 1980s is in large part the work of engagé male intellectuals: a passionate articulation of mostly political themes. At their best, these poems speak truth to power with rhetorical grandeur and sophistication. Thrilling invective, often directed at the State and its agents, alternates with passages of eloquent lamentation, a reckoning with the failures and tragedies of contemporary Arab history. There are also love poems of great sensuality, lyrics that activate a tradition of erotic literature dating back to the pre-Islamic period. Even in these comparatively intimate poems, however, the specter of political battles is rarely absent. The verse of Mahmoud Darwish, Adonis, and Nizar Qabbani—three Arab poets who have been extensively translated into English—is the verse of latter-day prophets, a poetry whose dominant modes are those of denunciation, celebration, and grief.

To move from that body of poetry to the work of Iman Mersal is an exhilarating if also disorienting experience. After the icy heights of rhetoric, we are plunged into a warm and fast-moving verbal river. Mersal's poetry is often ironic in tone, teetering between confessionalism and faux-confessionalism, between sarcasm and sadness, and full of unexpected leaps of logic and imagery. "The thread of the story fell to the ground so I went down on my hands and knees to hunt for it," one poem begins, turning a figure of speech into a real object, as though language itself might wriggle into life at any moment. It isn't that Mersal's poetry avoids politics, but she finds it in unexpected places: not in the public square or at the checkpoint, but rather in the realm of sexual relations, commonplace idioms, and hierarchies of power that are more durable because mostly unacknowledged.

Although Mersal's poems don't often deal with historical events, and even go out of their way to avoid them—"Map store," for example, is partly a meditation on 9/11, though it never mentions the attacks—they are nevertheless importantly marked by circumstances. Born in 1966, in the small town of Mit 'Adlan in the Nile Delta, Mersal published her first poems at a historical moment of ideological exhaustion. The fall of the Soviet Union coincided in the Arab world with a withering of hopes for Palestinian liberation, the rise of violent Islamism, and Arab nationalism's last gasp in the grotesque dictatorship of Saddam Hussein. In Cairo, the rule of Hosni Mubarak ground into its second decade, devoid of any raison d'être other than the remorseless repression of dissent. Worse, the regime claimed for itself the language of democracy, human rights, and modernization. Mersal's discovery of meaningful politics outside organized parties and within the interstices of everyday life is, in this context, very much of its time. So is her wariness toward familiar forms of collective mobilization, whether in the name of nation, party, or class. The sensibility at work in her poems is defiantly singular and skeptical.

The discovery of inequality in the everyday realms of sex, work, and child-rearing has long been a signature of feminist politics, and Mersal is keenly attuned to the ways that patriarchy shapes even our most intimate utterances (see, for example, "A man decides to explain to me what love is," a poem written many years before Merriam-Webster adopted *mansplain*). As a student at Mansoura University in the late 1980s, she co-edited the feminist magazine *Bint al-ard* (Daughter of the earth), in which she published some of her earliest work. But Mersal is chary of the self-righteousness and stale phrasemaking that come from conflating one's poetry with one's politics. She doesn't presume to speak for any collective, yet by digging into and exposing the most personal matters—sexual infidelity, mental illness, ugly feelings—she ensures that her poems will rhyme with the experience of others, in the Arab world and elsewhere. While acknowledging the pull of friendship and solidarity, these poems keep coming back to the task of telling one's own story, especially the most difficult and unheroic parts.

The poems in this volume are selected from Mersal's four collections of verse, stretching from the mid-nineties to the present. Mersal's first two books, *Mamarr mu'tim yasluh li-ta'allum al-raqs* (A dark alley suitable for dance lessons; 1995) and *Al-mashi atwal waqt mumkin* (Walking as long as possible; 1997), trace the itinerary of a personal and literary education. These are poems that react, with varying degrees of impatience and anger, against the conventions of Arabic poetry, and of Egyptian intellectual life more broadly. Mersal's early work was not welcomed by the almost entirely male literary establishment, whose sway over cultural matters is close to absolute. The gatekeepers, who often plume themselves on their enlightened views and public stances, found Mersal's aggressive ironies politically suspect. No doubt they felt the personal sting of poems like "Respect for Marx" or

"The State," which suggest how left-wing politics, for many male intellectuals, had become a license for boorishness and timid posturing. Nor had they ever read an Arab poet writing about cheating, suicide, and self-loathing in this way. Not because the things hadn't existed, of course—they were right in front of everyone's eyes—but because they had never been recognized as subjects for poetry.

Mersal's relations with the older generation of female intellectuals were only slightly less contentious. The poem "Amina," for example, stems from a trip to Baghdad that Mersal made in 1992 in the company of other Egyptian feminists, in solidarity with Iraqi women in the aftermath of the first Gulf War. While in Baghdad, she shared a hotel room with one of her mentors, Amina Rachid, the granddaughter of an Egyptian prime minister and an underground leftist in her youth, who had studied at the Sorbonne and become a professor of French at Cairo University. Mersal's poem about their brief episode as roommates, while affectionate and admiring, makes clear the divide between this cosmopolitan aristocrat of the Left and a young outsider who felt like she had no room to breathe. Mersal knows the rejection of decorousness can easily become an excuse for self-indulgence ("confessional" poetry always takes this risk), and her own poems are better read as interrogations of the impulse to make one's private life into a public spectacle. They ultimately take the self not as an object to be displayed but as a constantly shifting terrain for exploration.

In retrospect, one sees that Mersal's early poems are in many ways dependent on the social and literary strictures they so intelligently defy. They are declarations of independence that define themselves against a world of customs they seek to abandon, or explode. Mersal's farewell to the era of her youth is "The threshold," a valedictory poem about Cairo in the nineties, crowded with Europeanizing elites, posturing poets, and entitled State intellectuals. Like many other Beat or Beat-influenced long poems, from Allen Ginsberg's "Howl" to Roberto Bolaño's "Los neochilenos," "The threshold" is a poem of the open road that also tells the story of a generation. (In Egypt, Mersal is often associated with the "generation of the nineties," a literary grouping known for its sly nonconformism and its disillusionment with conventional politics; one of its members, the poet Osama al-Danasouri, appears in several poems collected here.) Mersal's merry bohemian band wends its way from the Opera House in Zamalek, Cairo's poshest neighborhood, to the ministry buildings and bars of downtown, teeming with would-be intellectuals, through the streets of Old Cairo, and out into the vast necropolis of the City of the Dead, a burial ground that is also a point of departure.

In 1998, Mersal married the musicologist Michael Frishkopf and moved to Edmonton, Canada, where she took a job teaching at the University of Alberta and they raised two boys. In her third collection, *Jughrafiya badila* (Alternative geography; 2006), and most powerfully in her latest, *Hatta atakhalla 'an fikrat al-buyut* (Until I give up the idea of home; 2013), Mersal moves beyond gestures of defiance to establish a sensibility entirely her own, and unique in Arab letters. She has left behind the Cairo of her youth to write about the melancholy comedy of working and raising a family in a foreign country, a place where the animosities that once provoked her into poetry are suddenly hard to find. "Why did she come?" is Mersal's first meditation on this displacement, and a turning point in her poetry. It imagines the transportation of a "mummy" into the New World of suburban ennui, organic foods, and immigrants of all kinds. Mersal wonders anxiously whether her new life might lack the needed irritants. "It's hard to meet a classical Communist," she grouses of Canada. "Nothing here deserves your rebellion." But in fact expatriation provided Mersal with new subjects: the conflicted feelings of emigrants toward the old country, their struggles to reconcile themselves with the new, the very idea of home.

Classical Arabic poetry includes a genre called *al-hanin ila-l-awtan*, a yearning for the homeland. In a typical example, the poet (often a courtier in exile) laments his present state, remembers the graces of his native environment—its flora and fauna, his family and friends—and expresses a wish to return before he dies. Mersal's later poetry resonates with this ancient genre, but subjects its nostalgias to withering scrutiny. She carries the tradition forward in the form of a critique, or betrayal. (Mersal's interest in infidelity should also be seen in this light: betrayal is needed to make things new; it is an artistic principle as much as a political and an erotic one.)

In an important poem, "The curse of small creatures," Mersal returns to her native village of Mit 'Adlan no longer an anxious and angry adolescent but an anthropologist of her former self, a camera-toting outsider who looks back on her childhood in a series of snapshots that she both recognizes and struggles to decipher. This *cahier d'un retour au pays natal* is a work of summation and literary maturity; it stands in relation to Mersal's oeuvre somewhat in the way that Adrienne Rich's "Diving into the Wreck" stands in relation to hers. Iman is a careful reader of Rich, and it is not by chance that in both works, the poet grabs a camera and plunges into her past, trying to see beyond the comforting myths in order to reckon with what Rich calls "the damage that was done / and the treasures that prevail."

All of Mersal's poems were originally written in prose—sometimes with line breaks, sometimes without. In Arabic, this verse form is called the *qasidat al-nathr* (prose poem); it is a relatively recent development, dating from the late 1950s. The form represented an important, even revolutionary change: until the mid-twentieth century, Arabic poetry was composed in fixed meters and line lengths, more or less unchanged for fourteen hundred years. But while the pioneers of the *qasidat al-nathr*—particularly the Syrian poet Adonis—still wrote in a high poetic register, Mersal's prose poems are emphatically prosaic, not only in their subject matter but also in their diction, rhythm, and tone. Where Adonis took as his model the French poet Saint-John Perse, a writer of classical eloquence and poise, Mersal's affinities lie with poets such as Charles Simic and Wislawa Szymborska, with whom she shares a mistrust of bombast and an interest in the everyday surreal. Like these writers, Mersal has an extraordinary sensitivity to the ways in which State officialese has distorted the common language, turning phrases like "the people" into clichés that poets can now handle only with very long tweezers. Mersal's commitment to the prosaic is one way to fight this debasement, to rescue everyday life—the realm of wasted days—and its idioms from the dead hand of officialese.

My versions of these poems have benefited more than I can say from long and detailed conversations about them with Mersal. Translations, like hot air, tend to expand, but Mersal's distinctive tone of voice is economical and even, at times, austere. Although she writes in prose, her poems have a formalist stringency, an animus against flabby language and sloppy sentiment alike. Her alertness to these flaws, even in English, has strengthened my renderings and also, I hope, made their music more like the originals'. Most of our conversations took place over Skype, which allowed Mersal to smoke in her study in Edmonton while we worked. In an early poem, she wonders whether such an elegant-sounding name as *Iman Mersal*—in Arabic, it has connotations of flowing ease and looseness—could possibly be attached to a person with such raspy lungs. That singular and strangely mellifluous rasp has been the tuning fork for my English versions.

THE

THRESHOLD

SELF-EXPOSURE

I should tell my father
the only man who shattered me
with desire looked just like him.

I should tell my friends
how many photos I have of myself,
each representing the real me,
which I'll send to them one by one.

I should tell my lover,
Be grateful for my infidelities.
Without them I wouldn't
have stuck around long enough
to discover the open window in your laugh.

As for me,
I'm pretty sure
my self-exposures
are for me to hide behind.

AMINA

You order beers on the telephone
with the confidence of a woman
who speaks three languages
and ties her words in colorful knots.

Where did you get this calm assurance
as if you'd never left your father's house?
How do you always intimidate
without intending to?
What is this magnetism
that draws me out of myself?
And what is it with me
that when a hotel room
offers me the perfect friend
I hurl in her face
my usual vulgarities,
the coarseness I'm so fluent in?

Go ahead, be shocked.
I'm a fair-minded person.
I'll give you more than half the air in the room
so long as you see me for what I am.

You're twenty years older than my mother
and wear bright colors
and never go gray.

My perfect friend,
why don't you get out now?
Then I could climb into
your silver-colored suitcases
and try on your elegant outfits.
Why don't you get out
and leave all the oxygen to me?

The empty space you leave behind
might make me bite my lips in regret
as I ponder your toothbrush,
wet and familiar.

I HAVE A MUSICAL NAME

Maybe it was the window I sat next to
that promised some unusual glory.
In my notebooks I wrote *Iman:*
Student at the Iman Mersal Elementary School
and neither the teacher's long stick
nor laughter from the back rows
could persuade me otherwise.

I considered lending my name to our street,
so long as its houses were enlarged
and secret rooms built
for my girlfriends to smoke in bed
without worrying about older brothers.

After the roofs are smashed to ease the pressure
on the walls, the dead grandmothers' slippers, pots,
and empty jars—which after long service
the mothers packed away—would be shipped off.
Doors would be painted orange
as a symbolic expression of joy
and peepholes would replace doorknobs so that
anyone could look in on the boisterous families
and no one on our street would be lonely.

Bold experiments
are the product of great minds
is how passersby might speak of me
as they stroll the sparkly sidewalks
of the street that bears my name.
But because of an old grudge between us
(its stones had left marks on my knees)
I decided the street didn't deserve the honor.

I don't remember when I discovered that I had
a musical name, a name suitable for signing
at the bottom of lyrical poems
and for waving in the faces
of friends with ordinary names
who couldn't grasp the true meaning
of bearing such an ambiguous one,
sowing unease all around
and inviting you to become someone else
when new acquaintances ask
Are you a Christian? or
Are you part Lebanese?

But something must have gone wrong.
Because now when someone calls to me
I get confused and look all around.
Is it possible that a body like my body
and lungs like these—growing raspier

by the day—could have a name like that?
I often see myself
moving between bedroom and bathroom
without the benefit of a whale's stomach
to get rid of what I can't digest.

THE CLOT

FOR MY FATHER

JUST SLEEPING

His lips twist in anger
at something he no longer remembers.
He sleeps deeply,
hands under his head,
like the conscripts of Central Security
in their late-night trucks,
eyes closed against all they've seen,
breathing in sync with the engines,
transformed all at once into angels.

ELECTROCARDIOGRAM

I should have been a doctor
so I could read the EKG
and confirm the clot was just a cloud
dissolving into ordinary tears
with the next warm gust of air.
But I'm of no use to anyone.
My father, who can't sleep anywhere but his own bed,
is in the middle of an enormous ward,
deeply asleep on a table.

WAILING

Wordless women
line the hallways leading to your bed,
ritually preparing themselves
to scrape the accumulated rust from throats
that never make a sound
except when they wail together.

A GOOD SIGN

A man in the next bed
is carried out by volunteers
to the common graveyard.

For you, this is a good sign.
Death will certainly not come back
to the same room in the same night.

PORTRAIT

His heart hung on every step I took and yet
he left behind only a familiar, musty smell.
He may have hated my short pants
and my unmusical poems
but I caught him more than once
swept up in the noise of my friends
and dizzied by the smoke they left
in their wake.

SIMILARITY

So that I could afford an anthology of foreign poetry,
this man, now deep asleep, convinced me
his wedding ring was too tight for his finger
and didn't stop smiling as we left the jewelers' district
even when I said there was absolutely no similarity
between his nose and mine.

I GREET YOUR DEATH

I'll greet your death as merely
the last thing you did to me
and won't enjoy the relief I expected,
feeling that you've taken away
any chance to diagnose
the tumors that grew between us.
In the morning, I might be
surprised by swollen eyelids
and a knot in my back
that gets tighter and tighter.

HOUSE OF MIRRORS

We'll go to the amusement park
and enter its house of mirrors,
so that you can see yourself taller than your father's palm tree,
and see me next to you, short and humpbacked.
No doubt we'll laugh a lot
and forgiveness will go both ways,
each knowing the other
also carried on their back the weight
of a childhood with no trips
to the amusement park.

VISITS

My dead mother often visits in dreams,
sometimes wiping from my nose
what she thinks is schoolyard dirt,
sometimes doing my braids
with tough and practiced hands,
but unable to see the scissors
that would subjugate my unruly hair
and just as blind to its hacked-off ends.

You too
might stop the world's turning when you die,
which would give me enough time
to open your eyes.

MANY TIMES

Many times the doctor
came into our house and said,
"You waited too long."

This is why
I erase the medical histories of loved ones
who aren't buried when they die,
and why I tell the windows of my room
while shutting them firmly
that I have my reasons for mourning
when neighbors play loud music.

MISTAKE

I tie my hair back
to look like a young woman you loved long ago,
always rinse away the taste
of my friends' beer
before coming home,
and never say anything about God in your presence.
So there's nothing you need to forgive me for.
You're a good man. But it was a mistake to make me
think that the world is like a school for girls
and that I should set aside my desires
just to be first in the class.

NEUTRALITY

I'll throw away all the reassuring lies
and destroy while he watches
the clay I molded to fit his dreams.
As for him,
he'll point to the left side of his chest,
and as for me,
I'll nod my head with a nurse's neutrality.

He needs to know
while he clings to his coma
that his desire to die
won't hide the family's fractures.

LITTLE LOCKERS

The windows are always gray
and generously proportioned,
allowing those in bed
to follow the traffic
and weather conditions outside.

The doctors always have aquiline noses
and spectacles
that establish the distance between them and pain.

Relatives always leave roses
at the room's entrance
asking forgiveness from the dead-to-be.

Women always wander the hallways
without makeup
while sons stand under bright lights
clutching X-rays
and promising to stop being so spiteful
if only their parents are granted a little more time.

Everything repeats itself.
The little lockers fill up with new bodies
like a perforated lung, inhaling the world's oxygen
and leaving all these other chests
to suck the wind.

It's unlikely
I'll take my father to the shore at the end of the year,
and so
I'll hang at the foot of his bed a picture
of crowds at the beach
and shorelines that recede into the unknown.
It's unlikely he'll see it,
and so
I'll hold my breath
as I wet his fingertips with salt water,
and later I may even come to believe
I heard him say
I smell the scent of iodine.

Rumormongers with low self-esteem
Lovers of cheap weed and awkward confessions
Anti-State agitators
Theorists of infidelity
Genealogists who dig up family trees
looking for less forgettable names
Reformers on the inside
People straightforward as garbage
Pessimists who keep their hands clean
Kind souls because there's no alternative
People like me

Those worthy of my friendship,
those whom you created for me,
are abundant this year.
Please, God,
take back your blessings,
but don't break your promise
of fresh enemies.

A NIGHT AT THE THEATER

The man on the bus
who cursed our driver for missing his stop
now sings under a lofty balcony,
looking skinny in his fake hair.
His eyes are smaller than I remember.

How did he fall in love with Juliet in less than an hour
while his own wife
(she let everyone know she was his wife)
fights off yawns in the front row
and waits for the play to end?

Juliet was born a very long time ago.
With some help from the stage lights
and her white dress, she looks sad,
and indeed we all know she's about to die.

Why doesn't the cameraman take a step
back from the body?
The way he's doing it
everyone will see
how hard she's trying not to breathe.

Now members of the two households
remove their stiff costumes,
put away their daggers, and hunt
for trousers and watches.
Some will dash to the bathroom
before going out to take their bows.

If I were Romeo
I'd keep the suicide scene short
so as not to hear
my wife's snoring.

SOLITUDE EXERCISES

He sleeps in the next room with a wall between us.
I'm not being metaphorical
about the wall.
I could hang photos of my lover on it,
pictures of him smoking or thinking,
so long as I found a neutral place for them
out of respect for the distance between us.

Apparently God doesn't love me.
I'm old enough to know it for sure:
God hasn't loved me for a long time,
ever since he fell for the math teacher
on whom he bestowed sharp eyes
and chalk pieces of many colors
and opportunities to torment a little girl like me
who couldn't define the relation
between nonsequential numbers.
Anyway, it isn't important whether God loves me.
No one in this world—not even the goody-goodies—
can prove that God loves them.

I know how to open a door and close it behind me
softly, so as not to wake my lover.

There's nothing dramatic
about a girl heading down to the street
with no place to go.

When Dostoyevsky said
Everyone needs a home, a somewhere they can go
he was talking about classical people
who wore their sideburns long
and overcoats like loneliness.
I don't like drama
and don't see the point in ruining a rose
just to suit the dearly departed.

If I ever get out of this room
I'll grab the hand of the first fellow I meet
and make him accompany me to a side-street café.
I'll tell him there's a man sleeping peacefully
in the room next to mine, a man
whose biggest ideas wouldn't fit around my pinkie, a man
who has failed to be my wastebasket even once
and lets everything spill into the street.
I'll tell him that I'm an orphan
(I used to think this was what makes good poems,
which is precisely why they weren't)
and that I don't take good care of myself
to the point where a little sinus inflammation

is on the verge of becoming cancerous (and I won't stop there).
The decent thing is for you to act like an angel before you die
so that friends have no trouble coming up with
dignified adjectives to describe you,
but I'll tell him that if he leaves me
death would be easier
than moving my right foot.

In the side-street café
I'll tell the fellow I've just met many things all at once.
I'll lay the traps of my voice
for his atavistic desire to be helpful
and perhaps he'll even take me home and wake his wife,
whom I'll smile at as she moves
across the filthy kilim toward me,
feigning shyness to reassure her
and make her proud of her husband.
He'll suggest that I wipe the slate clean and start over
while I promise to take up a musical instrument
(something plausible for my small size) and to meet him again
at one of those wonderful patriotic extravaganzas.

I've threatened everyone who loves me
with death if I lose them,
but I don't plan to die for anyone else's sake.
Suicides—of this I've no doubt—

have more faith in life than they should
and believe it's waiting for them somewhere else.

I swear I won't leave this room until he dies in front of me.
Then I'll put my ear to his chest:
a silence that can't be contradicted
even by a cat with the claws of a thwarted woman
who attempts in her hysteria to overturn the wastebasket
filled with the remains of our afternoon together—
the very wastebasket
I habitually place at the top of the staircase
to prove to the neighbors that I have a decent family.

I'll squeeze your fingers and examine you
like a surgeon who needs no scalpel
to dig out the boil.
I'll put your fingers in a bowl of ice
and when they stop trembling
I'll leave this place, swaddled in loss
and light on my feet.

You really need to die in front of me.
The death of loved ones is a unique opportunity to look for
    substitutes.
Riding the East Delta Railway, I would select a likely

woman, one who would open for me
the treasure chest of her big heart
upon hearing of my mother's death when I was six years old.

The truth
is that I was seven
but *six* seems so much more pathetic.
(Middle-aged mothers are devoted to sorrow,
maybe to justify wearing black so soon.)
These little retouches
have a magical effect
totally incomprehensible to those
who haven't had to steal kindness from strangers.

DESCRIPTION OF A MIGRAINE

I wanted to describe my chronic migraine
as one piece of evidence
that the chemical processes
occurring in my wonderful brain
were working effectively.

I intended to begin
My two hands aren't enough to prop my head up
but wrote instead:
A bullet from an unseen gun rips into
peaceful dimness
complete disorientation
fracture
a thousand separate splinters—
and also the pleasure
of arousing the sore spots
simply by remembering them.

RESPECT FOR MARX

In front of brightly lit windows
overflowing with lingerie
I can't stop myself
from thinking about Marx.

A respect for Karl Marx
is the one thing my lovers had in common.
I allowed all of them, though to differing extents,
to paw at the cotton dolls
hidden in my body.

Marx
Marx
I'll never forgive him.

IT SEEMS I INHERIT THE DEAD

After I walked back among all the large shoes
from my mother's burial
leaving her to tend her chickens in some obscurer place
it was my job to protect our house from the neighbors' spying
and I got used to sitting on the doorstep
waiting for the heroine—the one they always treated badly—
of the radio serials.
The day my friend received a visa
to try out her body on a foreign continent
(and although she hadn't forgotten, as she usually did,
her cigarettes on my table)
I decided that smoking was henceforth necessary
and soon I had a private drawer
and also a mysterious man
who was in fact my friend's former lover.

And one day
when doctors fail to find a kidney
Osama's body doesn't reject—
Osama,
whose kidneys shrivel

because he represses his bitterness for the sake of elegance—
I will use his thumbprint
while talking to prove I'm here.

It seems I inherit the dead,
and one day
I'll sit by myself in a café
after the death of all those I loved
without any feeling of loss
because my body is a large woven basket
where they have left
their traces.

A VISIT

It's best to regulate your breath
on the way up
by pausing briefly on landings.
On the way down
just hold on to the balustrade
so that you don't fall.
When you're back on the street,
try to keep your head up
and not look back.

*

The one behind the door
should open it as quickly as possible
before the one outside
has time to ponder what rationalizations
brought her here.

Time typically disappears
as one walks over the threshold.

*

At first the air seems heavier
the room darker
or more spacious than expected.
A painting might prompt a question
(*Who painted that?*)
so eyes scan the room
for an excuse to look interested.

*

A whetted ax cut the camphor tree
and after a year or so in the sun
here they are—shelves on a wall
filled with books and tchotchkes
providing the authors
a resting place to match their dreams
and protecting great minds from moths
but most importantly
allowing us to fill the first few minutes talking
about our shared intellectual interests.

How would it be if I sat over there?

*

We walk toward disaster with our eyes open
and no hesitation.
With a strength born of fear we pluck

the thorn that rankled our friendship,
confident that translated novels
provide aesthetic justification
for infidelity.

*

We'll arrange a happy coincidence
and each will be convinced
that a mysterious wind blew their clothes off
that their limbs
did no more than satisfy
the instinct to entwine.
We'll arrange a coincidence,
because scruples are a luxury of the strong,
and we'll refrain from gloating
with the aplomb of assassins
who arrive at the scene of the crime
and feel no need to make pleasantries.

*

I'll give you what my wife never discovered.

I won't give you what I couldn't offer him.

*

He was surprised by her terrible thinness
and noted how fair—almost translucent—her skin was.

The ardor hidden between her shoulder blades he said
was a peculiarly modern expression of femininity.

She let her vocal cords make their delirious vibrations
while wondering whether the real harvest
would be these green shoots
once they wilted.

*

There, attached to the dialysis machine
for six straight hours
with all the other patients around me
flat on their backs, apparently unresentful,
I thought about how to know you better
beyond our exchange of ideas and memories.

Two times a week
I'm washed by the machine's waters
and once the nausea is gone,
I smoke much better.

Have you read Justine?
You should, sweetie!
But we won't lose anything
that's beyond our capacity for loss.

*

He draws the curtains
so the light from across the street won't come in.
The darkness is complete and essential.
The darkness is final and concrete.
I press my fingers to my temples on the verge
of screaming at people who are very far away.

*

Someday I'll confess to them
in a quavering voice that suits
an encounter one is proud to have survived.
It will be wonderful
to open up the emotional veins of my friends—
veins that comfort has temporarily narrowed—
with all the details I wish had happened.

I won't tell anyone
that I hid from you the old scar on my knee
the scar
my lover would kiss, ritually
before weeping.

*

Your balcony touches your neighbor's balcony
and the dishes in your kitchen are spotless.
I'm sorry to be so familiar.

The wife
gathers laundry from the clothesline
and treads over the carpet's flowers—
flowers that might still be wet
with the breath of two bodies that never had enough time
and so took pleasure in their mounting terror.

SOME THINGS ESCAPED ME

One day I'll walk by
the house I lived in for years
without thinking about how far it is from my friends' houses.
The widow who woke me at night with her moans of pleasure
isn't my neighbor anymore.

I'll invent methods to make sure I'm not distracted,
like counting steps,
or biting my lips to enjoy the tender sting,
or busying my fingers with ripping apart a whole packet
of paper handkerchiefs.

I won't look for side roads
to avoid the pain.
I won't forbid myself to casually loiter
while training my teeth to chew
the cud of hatred.
I'll try to reconcile myself with the cold hands
that pushed me toward that house
by remembering how I never
soiled the bathroom's whiteness
with my distinctive kind of darkness.

No doubt some things escaped me.
These walls never entered my dreams,
so I never wondered what color of paint
might suit the unhappy glare.

This house where I lived for years
wasn't a student dormitory
for me to leave my one good dress
on a nail behind the door,
or hang my old photos with sticky tack.

I wonder if the sentimental quotations
I copied out from *Love in the Time of Cholera*
have settled there now in a heap of words
that reads like an absolute farce.

THE STATE

One head sends commands to all these hearts, limbs, and reproductive organs—a national army is made of absolutely headless individuals—and this generation no one needs, burning the public libraries and banishing depraved music from the local radio stations, its best and brightest volunteering to create a registry of streetwalkers so the State can make sure everyone pays their income tax while national anthems blare from public bathrooms to public squares and the distinguished opposition gathers beneath its banners to form a limited liability company for the enlightenment of the masses and meanwhile you lean over the balcony, peering down into the dark streets, biting your nails.

LOVE

After years of observing it from the window
or stashing it in a backpack with Xanax,
love explodes in the least likely place.
This scenario isn't innocent of literary designs.
It's like rubbing rust off the word *love*
or wiping away all the song-spittle
from *ardor* and *longing* and *lovesickness.*

If you happen to be an Arab poet
you must have written something about it by now.
You must have been lost for many years
in the desert of infatuation
hunting a mythical beast that guards the only well
so you can kill it, then weep
over the crime you were fated to commit
for a sip of water.
And even after you've returned to your people—
you're still a poet!
Love has a bad reputation.
Love is absolutely the worst thing there is to write about.

I look for the Muse in every poem I read.
The poet hangs her on a wall, nailed and spread-eagled,

the object of fantasy. We begin with the victim's eyes and end—
depending on how avant-garde our poet is—between her legs,
or, in the best case, with sympathy for her victimhood.
I played that role from time to time
but fortunately never met a truly great poet
and so emerged from these experiences with a hatred of
    Muses.

A chiffon bridge
you have to cross to reach the other shore—
though of course it isn't really any safer there
and you won't arrive on the other shore as yourself,
because you'll fall right away into some nasty pool
and many hands will offer to pull you out:
the hands of friends who think they've been there before,
poets whose vocation it is to witness your fall,
a bored insomniac psychoanalyst.
God's hand is not among them, but fear not—
fingers will presently reach out from an advertisement
for beauty products, promising you such smooth skin
that you'll never fear to fall again.

Love makes us authentic and narcissistic,
narcissistic in our authenticity and authentic in our narcissism,
    and so on.
There's no such thing as enough

until the arrival of he who said
contentment is an inexhaustible treasure
as if to set the senses' temperature at zero degrees
while he walks off into the desert
whistling something mystical like *I am you and you are me.*

THE THRESHOLD

It's true
the conductor's bow tie
—like arrowheads pointing at each other—
had already begun to droop
and we never saw the musicians' fingers
though we watched them exit one by one.
We knew the early-arriving poets
had a thing for the flute
despite its complete and utter sadness
and made a point of smoking during intermissions.
None of that interested us.
What we wanted to see was the black curtain
falling over the stage.

We were late—
just in time to see the fancy people
reclaiming their overcoats.
The mood was more or less oppressive
as in a military barracks
where you're forced to sing the national anthem,
or a foreign film, although in that case it would be raining.

We didn't mind that the concert was over
and instead of unraveling the denouement to the other shore
we just walked across the bridge,
saluting a man selling party hats
coming back from the moulid of Hussein.

It's true
I was separated from the others by a parade of camels
emerging from the Arab League.
When we found each other again
we offered our cigarettes to a security guard
who didn't know the name of the building he guarded
and finally arrived at a bar in the heart of the city
having broadened our horizons and earned a few scratches.

We had to sit there four years,
so we read Samir Amin
and Egyptianized Henry Miller
and Kundera gave us new ways to justify infidelity.

It was there we received a letter from a friend living in Paris
who told us that he'd discovered inside himself
a different person from the one he'd always known
and that he was dragging his misery behind him
over sidewalks much softer than Third World sidewalks
and going to pieces rather comfortably

and so for several months we envied him
and wished they would exile us as well to some foreign city.

We didn't panic when our money ran out
because one of us had become a Sufi
and after he offered up a short prayer
there opened beneath our feet—I swear to God—
a well full of beer
whereupon we behaved like people who've lost their minds
creating a private dictionary with words like
riwish
hinini
awaq
danasheen et cetera.

We screamed very loudly
and were understood by no one.

When the oldest of us suggested
that we become more forward-thinking
I conceived of a way to convert public toilets
into stalls for weeping
and public squares into urinals
and then all of a sudden
one long-serving intellectual screamed at his friend
When I'm talking about democracy

you shut the hell up
so we ran for it
until we could catch our breath on al-Mu'izz Street,
where we met a martyr with a frown
whom we reassured that he was actually alive
and could go on begging if he wanted
and also that there hadn't been a war in the first place.

It's true
we were about to nail down our relationship to metaphysics
when one of us began covering his skull
with an elaborate hat
making us all look like tourists
so that the spice vendor chased after us
saying over and over
Winnabi—stop!
For the sake of the Prophet—wait!

There was nowhere else to go but the City of the Dead.
We stayed there another year
wondering about the smell of guava
and when I decided to leave them all behind
and walk alone
I was already thirty.

BLACK FINGERS

Marrying a piano player
isn't like marrying a sailor—
something they all appreciate:
they'll never have to see you waiting at the port.
Instead, their last image of you
will be of a creature dangling from a rope
fingers splayed over her eyes
while her thin feet hang miles away
from the musical scales.

The grandmother said *Silly chicks are food for hawks*
The father said *Don't talk to strangers*
The professor said *East is East and West is West*
The friend from the café said *Leaving your homeland is a
    mistake that can only be fixed by never looking back*
The doctor said *You're expecting*

The doctor says *You're expecting*
and you say *No, I'm pregnant*
not because it's more feminine
and not because words are always unfair
but because *pregnant* is a word that feels full of itself,
which is exactly what you are.

THEY TEAR DOWN MY FAMILY HOME

As if sledgehammers weren't enough
the demolition men use their hands
to tear down the window jinn used to flit through
and with a kick the back door is gone. Its memory is gone.
Underfoot I feel the remains of the sugarloaves, oranges, and
    mangoes
our furtive visitors hid under their black shawls.
They would come after evening prayer,
the hems of their long gallabiyas
brushing across the threshold of the back door,
a door of gifts and sorceresses, now a door to nowhere.
The roof that never protected my childhood from the delta rains
has reverted to its old self—a few trees you can count on one
    hand.

Now they're tearing down her old bedroom, casting into the air
strands of her still-wet hair, hair that flies up from the cracks
of earthen walls about to become clods of dirt,
as if no one had ever rested their back there.
Did my mother bathe before bed or at dawn?
Did she pull her hair from the comb's teeth to ward off
the evil eye, or fire, or the stratagems of neighbors?

My mother's hair slips away like a gift, or retribution.

What ties me to her now?

I donated her dresses to charity because they didn't fit me.

If we met, I'd be her older sister.

What ties me to her now?

Her womb is with her in the ground—there

under the camphor tree, where early death is close enough to
    touch with your hand.

WHY DID SHE COME?

Why did she come to the New World? This mummy, this
  curiosity,
lying in state in her dusty linen, stuffed with life behind the
  museum's glass.
Maybe mummification is the opposite of immortality
since no mummy will ever give life to a rose.
The mummy didn't choose to emigrate, unlike those who wait
on long lines in embassies, build homes in foreign countries,
and dream of returning once they've turned into corpses.
You must take us back
is the legacy they hang around their children's necks
as if death were an identity
that can't be claimed until you're in the family plot.

*

Here too there are green trees,
stooped under the weight of snow,
and also rivers—though no lovers embrace on their banks,
thronged instead on Sunday mornings by joggers and their dogs
who never pause to look at the water, rigid with loneliness—
and immigrants unschooled as nature lovers
but convinced that pollution levels are lower here

and that chewing gelatin capsules of oxygen before bed
will lead to a longer life.

*

Why can't they forget they're from there?
These wretched outsiders
training their mouth muscles to disguise their accents—
accents like inherited diseases, exposing them
as soon as they get angry
and forget how to express their griefs in a foreign tongue.
Accents don't die but immigrants are good gravediggers.
They hang the names of dead family on the fridge
so as not to telephone them by mistake
and they pay a quarter of their salary on phone bills
to prove they live in a place very far from their childhood.
Why can't they forget?

*

The organic food is still unpurchased yet for the last hour
I've been staring at a photo of my mother
sitting on the doorstep of her father's house,
which no longer exists—
I mean the doorstep, though my mother doesn't either.
There's no one on the sidewalk. Cars come and go by remote
    control.

I bought this house with its vestigial doorstep
from the widow of a Spanish sculptor who built it on land
leased from Ukrainian immigrants
whom the Canadian government gave it to
after expropriating it from indigenous peoples to construct a city
with several universities, dozens of shopping malls,
and thousands like me who own remote-control cars
and understand the health benefits of organic food.

*

In just six steps, the lonely immigrant writes a model letter to
his family:
—he chooses a moment when he isn't missing them
—he sits with his back to the street since walls are more neutral
—he carefully distributes his *salaams*
—he recites the formulas he was raised on and never expected
to repeat, such as *I love you more than there are stars in the sky
or grains of sand on the shore* and *I dream of you as the thirsty
man dreams of water and the sick man dreams of a cure and
the stranger of his homeland*
—he says nothing of his actual life since he isn't sure how it
might be received
—he writes *thank God* many times to assure them of his faith

*

What you've learned here is no different from what you learned
    there:
—read for your passport away from reality
—hide anxiety with vulgar language
—banish weakness by growing your nails
—cure insomnia by smoking always and tidying your
    drawers sometimes
—use three different brands of eyedrops to clear your vision,
    then enjoy your blindness (even better is the moment when
    your eyelids close over the burn)
Here as well as there
life seems to exist only to be watched from afar.

*

A surprising peace enters your body.
Just let your head rest beneath the water.
Why not? This is your bright idea,
glistening like a pearl in the trash?
How can you throw it away like this?
It's your own idea, contrary, authentic.
These seconds don't pass one after another,
they are the razor's edge between moments.
You remember the dirty dishes in the kitchen,
the mail with its catalogs,
the lights drilling into your eyes . . .
The mercy you didn't know you were looking for is here.
It will slip into your lungs

if you let your body relax . . . sink to the bottom . . . stay down
  just a few seconds more . . .
There's no reason to be frightened.
Time makes no difference.
It isn't a weight dragging your courage down.
Time is nothing, time is just time.

*

You left your poor enemies on another continent
and feel ashamed whenever you think of them.
Nothing makes you angry anymore.
It's hard to meet a classical Communist here,
where clocks hang in government offices
rather than pictures of the president.
Perhaps these days of sedation are the real nightmare.
Nothing here deserves your rebellion.
You are content and you are dead.
The life around you is like the hand of mercy
turning up the room lights for an old blind man
so he can read the past.

MORNING BELL

The eye opens like a curtain rising
In the dark, feet search for something real
Consciousness hasn't happened yet
And the floorboards are skin temperature
A fresh repetition, today will be one more or one less
An impromptu concert strikes up in the kitchen
Maybe this black coffee is the morning bell—
the prize you win for returning safe from sleep.

C V

A ruthless catalog of sorrows:
years in front of the screen, diplomas before jobs,
and languages—all that torture—now ranged under *Languages.*
Where are all the wasted days? And the nights
of walking with hands stretched out
and the visions that crept over the walls?
Where are the feelings of guilt
and the sudden sadness faced with a little hill of fruit
atop a handcart in some forgotten street?
Years with no mention of the empty hours or the funerals,
expunged of black depressions and nibbled nails,
the house keys forgotten inside the house.
There isn't a single open window
and no trace of the desire, deferred, to leap out.
A life overstuffed with accomplishments,
scrubbed free of dirt:
proof that the one who lived it
has cut all ties to the earth.

A GRAVE I'M ABOUT TO DIG

As I return home with a dead bird in my hand, a little grave I'm about to dig waits for us in the backyard.

No blood on the washed feathers, two outspread wings, and a dewdrop (some concentrate of spirit?) on its beak, as if it had flown for many days while actually dead.

Its fall was fated in the Lord's eyes, heavy and diagonal in front of mine.

I'm the one who left my country back there to go for a walk in this forest, holding a dead bird whose absence the flock never noticed,

returning home for a funeral that might have been a solemn one were it not for the sneakers on my feet.

A LIFE

This didn't happen in my family home—no, not among those who know me (or so I once believed).

My life, the life I've never been able to touch, never been able to find a picture showing just the two of us—that life is next to me on my bed, opening her eyes after a long slumber and stretching her limbs, like a princess who knows that her father's palace is magically protected against thieves, and that even if the wars never seem to end, happiness lies just beneath the skin.

This is the life into which more than one father stuffed his ambitions, more than one mother her scissors, more than one doctor his pills, more than one activist his sword, more than one institution its stupidity, and more than one school of poetry its poetics.

My life that I've lugged with me from city to city, running out of breath while chasing it from school to library, from the kitchen to the bar, from the ney to the piano, from Marx to the museums, from the memory of a body's smell to the dream of an airport lounge, from everything that I don't know to everything that I don't know. My life, whose existence I've never been sure of, lies next to me on my bed, opening her eyes after a long slumber and stretching her limbs, like a princess who knows that her father's palace is magically protected against thieves, and that even if the wars never seem to end, happiness lies just beneath the skin.

This is how I awoke in that strange land the morning I turned forty, and if it weren't for the fact that God has never once chosen a woman, I'd have said it was the first sign of prophethood. If it weren't for my own peculiar way of thinking, I'd cite Mahmoud Darwish about *a woman who entered her forties with perfect apricots*, or else the words of Milosz: *I felt a door opening in me and I entered.*

I see before me a long line of the dead—dead, perhaps, because I loved them—and I see the homes designed for insomnia, which I always cleaned very carefully during the holidays, and the gifts I never opened, and the poems stolen from me line by line until I doubted whether they were ever mine, and men I only met at the wrong times, and clinics of which I remember nothing but the bars on their windows. I see my whole life before me and I could even embrace her if I wished, or sit on her lap and sing, or wail.

I DREAMT OF YOU

Where did he go?

Instead of house slippers, I stuffed my feet into your heavy shoes (and they really were yours). Then I stalked through Noah's boat in search of him. The kitchen was clean, the ashtray evidence of a smoker's hysteria, the door to the balcony wide open, and a breeze rustled pages on the floor. When did he leave? How did I fall asleep with my guest still sitting across from me on the sofa? How did his shoes get into my room and how could he have left for the big city in bare feet? When I couldn't find my father's black shoes in their usual place, I felt lost. Then I woke.

Reread Freud, X said. M said, *He stole the father's authority and left you a few clues about where he went.* N said, *Maybe he stole the desire for the father and left you his authority in the form of shoes too big for you to fill.*

A GIFT FROM MOMMY ON
YOUR SEVENTH BIRTHDAY

These are the instructions:

1. Spread a tablecloth on level ground.
2. Make sure to wear the provided goggles.
3. Grab the ax with your right hand.
4. Strike the hollow brick very lightly.
5. If you strike too hard, you might break the treasure hidden inside.

—I don't know what the treasure is either, but here's what's written on the box: *If you're lucky, a gift from the pharaohs lies inside!*

—No, sweetie, no one in Egypt sent this to you, it was made in China.

—Let's think. Could it be a mummy, with no internal organs? The Great Pyramid's tomb before the archaeologists discovered it? The head of Cleopatra after she fell in love?

—Those are just guesses . . .

—You won't know until you break it to pieces.

—Let's go out to the backyard first. If we do it here, everything will be covered in dust.

SOUND COUNSEL FOR GIRLS
AND BOYS OVER FORTY

After forty, a man counts the hairs caught in his comb every morning and a woman plucks the white ones before going to bed. A woman examines her nipples in the mirror for any change of color, while a man stares at them in public more and more intently. A woman's nightmares are about vaginal dryness, a man gets terrified by the swelling of his prostate.

The expert went on to say that it wasn't merely by such symptoms that we distinguish between the sexes. His investigations had determined that after forty a man becomes proud of the number of women he's brought to orgasm, while women regret how many times they've had to fake one. Naturally, a woman talks very little about such things, for she is as dark and secretive as a well, while a man who talks of them will light up like a boulevard with delight. But don't worry, my feminist friends: everyone listening to the man knows he's lying.

Some people believe that after forty they get closer to the truth, but I'm sorry to disappoint them. In fact, the truth is of interest to no one but children and the insane. While it's true that some men become prophets, let us not forget that most of their followers are women. It's also true that some females become wise women, but this is only to say that they become skilled in obfuscation. As for the poetess who claimed that after forty she entered *the stage of the butterfly*, I beg you not to understand her in the way of those who say *do not pray* while forgetting to cite the words that follow in the Quran (*while drunk*). For in the very next line the poetess says she flew at lightning speed along the straight and narrow path heading toward the light—the very light that prophets and wise women call, in their metaphorical fashion, *death*.

MAP STORE

Imagine him coming back from a war—
one of those wars that happen elsewhere
from which some people return with memories enough
to make a film that almost feels realistic—
coming back, as I say, from a desert in North Africa
and opening, with his newfound expertise in thirst,
a juice stand.
He was dropping some ice into those freshly squeezed
beverages which became at the end of the forties
an emblem of the new Pax Americana
when he discovered water puddling under the cooler.
He imagined a sea, a mainland, an island
and in this way there grew within him
the vague idea of what geography is.
Later, a grandson who had never been to war
converted the juice stand into a map store.

If you pass by some day
on a blocked artery in the heart of Manhattan
you'll see people who aren't from here
coming and going and rarely buying anything.
I once saw a woman brush some dust off a mountain

and a girl trail one of her braids over a lake
and I heard one man try to describe to another
the location of his distant house in a distant village
close to a distant city which appeared as a tiny dot
on the map of his distant country.

I pass by this place
not to share these strangers' griefs
nor to pour water into the Nile,
which appears as a motionless snake
on the map that hangs facing the door,
nor even to contemplate the aura that must have been there
just above the right knee of the store's original owner
whom I now see in a portrait wearing his uniform and medals
but with no sign of his wooden leg
and no trace of the water that leaked from his cooler.

To tell the truth, I don't know why I keep coming here,
but I can see now with my own eyes
the map seller
terrified, perhaps for the first time,
living through a war he couldn't sign up for—
because this time the war came to him.

THE CURSE OF SMALL CREATURES

They say a colony of ants devoured the walls and the birds. They say their ancestors migrated three times in two centuries. They say they filled in a swamp and built a house for God first, houses for the dead next, and finally houses for those who survived the curse of small creatures.

The place is called Mit 'Adlan, "Village of Justice," though it has seen plenty of injustice. The young people seem proud of the name and maybe names have lost their memories, we've gnawed at them with our teeth for so long. Mit 'Adlan is my own beautiful village, my native earth, and the subject of my nightmares.

Now its streets have names, even signs. Revolution Street, The Pharaohs, The Rightly Guided Caliphs. There's an arrow with the word *cemetery* written on it, which actually points to the cemetery. You can search for Mit 'Adlan on Google Earth. It looks like a broken watch left on a wall that used to hold up a house.

A village of tremendous secrets and empty doorways.

*

The men didn't ask God for anything, not openly, except for health and His protection. But God wasn't fooled, not in the mid-seventies. He kept an eye on their hopes, which stirred as they sipped their tea.

He watched the men leaving their homes, hands tucked behind their backs, clutching the hopes that were never spoken aloud, not even during evening prayer: Let brick walls replace earthen walls, let there be electricity instead of gas, may the first color TV be no less than twenty inches.

They may not have meant to deceive God, but He was not pleased.

When one built an addition, it smelled like burning gasoline—like rooms made for nightmares, with no angels climbing down the ladders, and a roof always under construction. One of them went to Iraq, where he died in a war others watched in full color.

Then one day the electricity arrived, just as they had hoped, and the survivors could string up lanterns to guide the mourners to the place of mourning.

*

A woman and a little girl, both bleached with acid. The woman doesn't smile (though she doesn't know she'll die exactly forty-seven days later) and the girl doesn't smile (though she doesn't yet know what death is). The woman has the girl's lips and forehead (the girl has the nose of a man who never made it into the photos). The woman's hand is on the girl's shoulder and the girl's hand is in a fist (she isn't angry, she's holding half a caramel). The girl's dress is not made from Egyptian cotton (Abdel Nasser, who made everything, died years ago), and her shoes are imported from Gaza (which is, needless to say, no longer a free-trade zone). The woman's watch doesn't work and she wears a thick belt. (Was this in style in 1974?)

*

They put the little boy in front of the camera and slip ten crisp guineas into his hand—although I should say, for precision's sake, that it was sometimes five. Click. The little boy cries out and the bills are suddenly gone. In the photo, he's still holding on; in the real world, the photographer took them back.

The hands of family newborns were always clutching money, all except Hosam, who wasn't afraid of the dark room or the camera's flash. He surprised everyone by swallowing the borrowed guineas and became a family legend—not for this, but because he drowned while fishing at the age of ten. Hosam, my friend! The way he sat at the back of class and chewed on his pencils embarrassed me. They took his picture out of the National Bank envelope, which had been in the Bata shoebox in the living room trunk, and put it in a silver frame. His death surprised no one. His nickname was *ibn mawt*, "son of death."

*

Whenever there was a funeral, all the men wore starched white gallabiyas, like extras in an advertisement for laundry detergent. The women, wearing black, slaughtered their fattest birds. The doors were open and the feasts were waiting—offerings to the god of death, so that he wouldn't return before the chicks were grown.

*

Here's a boy the army made a man. His ID card is in the pocket of his camouflage uniform. Instead of smoking amid the junk heaps and jinn of the storage room, risking his father's rage, here he is with the whole desert surrounding him. They gave him jackboots to march over his past. His childhood disappeared like water dripping from the holes of old shoes and he grew exactly two centimeters. There's a shovel under his arm. He dug a deep trench he never found time to take cover in. I don't know whom to thank for taking the picture, but it arrived at his mother's house—praise God—along with a wristwatch, the ID card, and the body.

*

When I got my first camera, I was already in the city, living on my own. I always brought it with me to Mit 'Adlan, as though without it I wouldn't recognize anyone. Watchful as a hunter, I waited for people to gather on a bench, for a housewife to dry her hands, for someone to change his gallabiya or to turn off the television. Then I flashed down—a divine intervention—to mark the unremarkable. How often I wished a fire or a war would start while my battery was still charged. I could kneel down in the rubble and snap pictures of people buried beneath the ruins. On some future visit, I would show them to the survivors so they might rejoice at having survived.

*

A day for airing out the living room and putting everything back in place. The smell of cleaning fluids, clothes drying on a line, the heat of noon. And then—hellfire from a mosque microphone, the men's siesta in the big room after lunch. On this blessed day, if no disaster strikes, gloomy creatures come visiting to complain of their bad luck and the soreness in their joints, creatures who slurp tea and praise God, who feel guilty when they forget their pains and laugh. Friday—a day I do not love.

*

The women look toasted by years in the sun. They examine you with furrowed brows.

They were pregnant more often than they should have been and miscarried on the way to the hospital—always on the way to the hospital. The babies who survived were born before dawn in rooms full of baked bread. In my family, children were like the harvest: one half went to the government.

Does this folded photo keep any trace of them? I put it

under the mattress, as my grandmother did with the photo of her son in the army. Here they are in front of me: anklets over their stockings, pants under short skirts, sleeves rolled up to display their bracelets, twists of braids still showing in the hair combed straight to their shoulders. They wore everything they owned, yet the smell of milk still slipped from under their clothes.

I can photoshop the creases away, but I can't crop my aunts out. They ask me with their eyes: *What will you do with us?* The studio photographer must have told them to smile and so they did, neither shyly nor boldly, without coquetry or exaggerated modesty. Even the roughness of their fingers is hard to make out in the glossy print.

This isn't what I remember of my aunts. How did they turn into symbols of Victorian Egypt? They were radiant on wedding nights, queens in darkened kitchens, and they grieved on the happiest holidays. What I remember isn't in the pictures, so why can I not let them go?

RAISING A GLASS WITH
AN ARAB NATIONALIST

The pianist was still droopy-eyed, her face as darkened as the keys they left her to press for half a century, though she must have been white as an angel when they first strung her up in the heavy frame on the wall.

Here amid the sighs of Umm Kulthum and the local wine of uncertain vintage, I thought my courage might walk through that door next to the bar. While the garçon read his tabloid and I slid among my options like a drop of dew on a bunch of grapes, an Arab nationalist made his entrance, hair completely white, as if he'd just been fighting off an invasion of the midan down the street.

"The nation is on fire," he said, instead of *good evening,* and I started coughing from the smoke that suddenly engulfed me.

Intermittent barks from outside covered the sounds of sighing inside. The garçon might turn up the volume a notch for the Nightingale of the East, but the bitch's howling will win the battle. She'll probably give birth to a couple of pups at least around the back of the building.

The garçon really should stop the 1943 Rivoli record. The composer, Zakariyya Ahmad, wouldn't approve of this medley of oud, dog barks, and coughing under a colonial-era roof.

I'd come back from a funeral that afternoon. A surgeon, just out of school, was waiting for me in a room he'd spent too much time tidying up.

But my courage never walked through the door—the sordid side door that separates the women's room from the men's urinal.

UP IN THE AIR

With my head on your shoulder
the flight attendant must have thought we were honeymooners
heading east over the ocean
sleeping peacefully with disheveled hair
hands folded on my chest
your shoulder as my pillow.
You carefully sipped your wine so as not to disturb
a woman whose name you didn't know.
I won't tell you that I've graded twenty papers on postcolonial
    literature,
cooked enough food to feed two children for a week,
and wrapped Walter Benjamin protectively in my underwear,
    not forgetting
to pack my computer, camera charger, and manuscripts,
all of which left my nerves so frayed that I fell asleep
on the shoulder of a man whose name I didn't know.
You and I are probably very much alike,
each with a full life, which nevertheless seems
at moments like these to have neither past nor future,
like a bottle of water drunk in a hurry and tossed away.

Don't ask me where I'm headed
just because you let me borrow your shoulder for five hours
or because you refrained, for my sake, from getting up to go
to the bathroom.
I might not have actually been asleep.

THE EMPLOYEE

She said to him, When a woman says *I'm a little drunk,*
this is actually a warning that she might collapse at any
  moment.
And when she tells you of a lost happiness
she means that you're responsible for giving it back to her
on a silver platter, like those knights in the stories of caliphs
who return home with the heads of enemies on their spears.
She continued, And when she sits next to you in the office
just as I'm sitting next to you right now
you must listen to her while placing your right hand on top
  of her left.

The woman spoke in rather husky tones,
which wasn't appropriate with a man like that, so wide-eyed,
but as for me, I sat and calmly listened
to these passionate words of wisdom
delivered by an employee to her colleague at work.

A MAN DECIDES TO EXPLAIN
TO ME WHAT LOVE IS

One day, a man decided to explain to me what love is. He was buttoning up his shirt while shadows gathered in the corners and the afternoon light crossed from one side of the room to the other. He seemed only half there, as when the screen dims and everyone in the movie theater starts looking for exit signs. It was then, glasses tidily fixed around the backs of his ears, that he decided to explain to me what love is.

In the half-lit room he murmured, "Love is actually a quest for . . . ," I opened my eyes and saw a band of conquistadors searching for gold in remotest Chile, hungry and dejected, while an Indian crouches behind a rock in fear. And when he said, "Love is being truly content with . . . ," I began to hear the voice of Ella Fitzgerald and pressed my fingers into a mound of black chocolate. And when he said, "It is a happiness which . . . ," well, I really couldn't imagine anything at all.

I'm sure I never saw that man again, because I never got to ask him if love is forgetting one's watch by the bedside.

Good morning, Imu. I've been online a few times but none of you guys have shown up—bastards. The time difference is a bitch, but what can you do.

All is good here. The thing I like best about what some call *the other world* is how far it is from Faisal Street. Imagine— no mosques or minarets, no Ministry of Culture, no public buses. And the women! All of them very pretty, and so kind that I haven't seen a single one wearing a veil in public.

I miss my trips to the dialysis clinic. When I asked the guards here, they just said *There is no illness after death.* Didn't I tell you? Now I can drink as much water as I like without worrying about how to get rid of it.

Anyway, sweetie, since you love me as much as you do, please read the attached. I was finally able to write a poem about our New Year's in 1992, though I can't tell if I really captured the mood of the party. "Away from it all with my friends" is the title God himself gave to me.

I planned to write about Yamani's brilliance and our painter friend's fingers when he pulled on his beard at the start of each sentence, and about Mohab's singing, and about Yasser on his chair in the corner observing the rest of us . . . But instead I wrote about Arwa Salih—she's in the other room, still sleepless—and about your back, Imu, as I see it from here, while you lean your arms on the balcony's rail. And also about that buzzing sound, a sound only I can hear, as I roll another joint to share with all my people stuck here waiting.

AN ESSAY ON CHILDREN'S GAMES

Many children's games depend on a physical handicap. Hopscotch, for example, requires a skillful player to hop from square to square on one leg while his other merely dangles in the air, as though amputated so long ago he had time to practice jumping without it.

Maybe I'm here on this continent simply to walk by myself for days, or years, as if no one there needed me, waited for me, asked about me, loved me, missed me, worried about me.

But hopscotch isn't the right metaphor because in fact, while I'm here, I do need all those people I wake up without and go to sleep without. Distance doesn't lessen the sense of guilt. *Guilt,* the word tolls inside me every time I remember that I'm *from there.* I've become more and more *from there* ever since I left. And guilt has been *eating at me* ever since I arrived, just yesterday, in this city perched over an ocean, to read some poems in some big theater and drink good wine with talented writers who aren't from there.

What does a person do who's come here to read some poems about there to people not from there, a person eaten by guilt even as she stands, as I do, on the balcony of a five-star hotel, lighting a cigarette and screaming or muttering curses, hoping that the police will haul her off to prison, hoping that something will happen to stop her from throwing herself off the seventh floor—and then, when there's a knock at the door, jumping under the bedcovers as though playing blindman's bluff?

In blindman's bluff, a player loses his sight and has to tag the others by patting the air or sniffing them out.

When a mother hides her face behind her head scarf, the infant believes, for a terrifying moment, that he's lost her forever. In most cases, fortunately, the mother quickly shows her face again, and in most cases the infant laughs louder and louder with each renewal of terror. I never did that with my children, maybe because when my mother died I was still in love with that game and kept waiting for her face to reappear.

It would be funny to think my relationship with children's games was determined by my mother's absence, and terrible to think her death is the reason I'm here, thirty years later, playing a game of peekaboo with everyone I want to be with.

My son would put his hands over his eyes, lying still in his bed and imagining he was invisible. He waited as long as he could, then took his hands away, ready for the surprise that, strangely, never dulled with repetition. He laughed at the success of his disappearing act, which never actually happened. Maybe I'm only here to wait for the expert player who will suddenly grab me and—to my surprise and delight—drag me back to where I belong.

When children pretend to be adults in their games there's always that one child who tells the others what to do. He doesn't always play a father or a math teacher. He might be a bus driver and decide who gets to ride, or a doctor who carefully selects his patients.

I don't remember playing any of those roles. I had one role and it never changed, like the oracles in ancient temples— that of the blind girl. A blind girl in math class, where my task was not to go up to the imaginary blackboard but to recite the multiplication tables from my seat on a bale of straw (whose task was to be a school bench). A blind girl, reciting the Quran at funerals and singing at weddings. A blind girl who doesn't play at blindman's bluff, who doesn't want to catch anyone, so that she might keep seeing no one as long as possible. A blind girl in every game of make-believe—the role no one wanted except me.

GOOD NIGHT

From your bed on another continent you say *good night*. You're going to sleep at eight in the morning, as the diligent novelist must, after a night of inventing plot twists, and after a long day, I extend my working woman's hand to sign the grocery receipt. Was it you who first said *We live the same moment in different time zones?*

I say *good night* with the same tenderness to the Indian woman standing since this morning behind the cash register, who smiles pleasantly as if she didn't at all resent last-minute customers.

I turn at the sound of your voice ringing out in the supermarket at closing time and see bananas sleeping in a little pile, grapes yawning in clusters, dewdrops on the apples, mushrooms radiating their inner warmth—and then the automatic door opens for me, for my body, surprised to occupy this sudden small space of emptiness.

ON EITHER SIDE OF THE DOOR

As soon as your finger touches the doorbell, it's chaos.
Blood rushes up my spine and into my ears
my feet stagger backward
each organ takes off in a different direction.

Ring the bell again.
Panting, patience exhausted, I make a point of dawdling,
as if sticking out my tongue at the time spent waiting for you.
Maybe these moments are more memorable than the next:
opening up for a man you wait for as he waits outside.
As if everything in the world were just fine,
my hands reach casually for the doorknob.

You cross the threshold.

You don't know what to do with yourself. I'll extend one hand
while the other plays with my glasses—
a conventional rich lady, a mistress of the salons
giving charity to orphans. *Please come in.*

You enter my home like Moses parting the waters,
crossing the sea to the desert.

The pharaoh's soldiers didn't catch you,
but it isn't fair that all those innocent horses drown,
or that the women of Egypt lose their gold forever.
You flee death into the wasteland,
no triumph to come and none behind,
foiling the Lord's designs once again.

I swear that dew dropped from the ceiling, softly,
like salt on my lips. Maybe that was why I never said
Please come in.
I gaze into the gloom of my home and am content.
The dim lighting gives me cover
while you sit there on the couch, exposed as a guest.

EVIL

I used to believe there was so much evil in the world,
and though I'm the gentlest of all my friends,
I never saw a rose in a vase without pinching the petals
between my thumb and index finger
to make sure it wasn't plastic.

But lately I've begun to doubt the existence of evil altogether
as if all the hurt in the world happens
at the moment we make sure
that the creatures we've made to bleed are real.

The thread of the story fell to the ground so I went down on my hands and knees to hunt for it. This was at one of those patriotic celebrations, and all I saw were imported shoes and jackboots.

Once, on a train, an Afghan woman who had never seen Afghanistan said to me, "Triumph is possible." *Is that a prophecy?* I wanted to ask. But my Persian was straight from a beginner's textbook and she looked, while listening to me, as though she were picking through a wardrobe whose owner died in a fire.

Let's assume the people arrived en masse at the square. Let's assume *the people* isn't a dirty word and that we know the meaning of *en masse*. Then how did all these police dogs get here? Who fitted them with parti-colored masks? More important, where is the line between flags and lingerie, anthems and anathemas, God and his creations—the ones put on earth to pay taxes?

Celebration. As if I'd never truly said the word before. As if it came from a Greek lexicon in which triumphant Spartans march home with Persian blood still wet on their spears and shields.

Perhaps there was no train, no prophecy, no Afghan woman sitting across from me for two hours. At times, for his own amusement, God leads our memories astray. What I can say is that from down here, among the shoes and jackboots, I'll never know for certain who triumphed over whom.

THE SLAVE TRADE

I went down the narrow passage, wide enough for one slave at a time, to the harbor.

An Englishman inspects the line of those leaving the fort— maybe he's unloaded his cargo of missionaries and guns and now waits for a ship to carry us over the ocean to the cane fields. A handsome man, to be honest. Why is he smiling at me?

Piles of gold beneath the palms, piles of salt under the sun.

When will a sailor come unfasten the iron ball from my feet? I want to make sure the pencil and Moleskine notebook are still in my backpack, since I plan to turn whatever happens to me into heart-wrenching prose.

"I was a good girl living with her aging parents . . . One day they went off to a funeral and I was left to look after our little hut. I would sing that old song, *I'll marry the one my heart desires,* and when a stranger kidnapped me the only sin I could remember was having eaten the meat my mother set aside for the gods. I knew it as soon as I put it in my mouth . . ."

I'll write about peeing while standing up, and sleeping while standing up, and weeping while standing up. I'll write about my body becoming my refuge, about the shit that became just shit once you got used to it. And I'll write . . .

Because I'll survive all the shipborne plagues
and the wounds unhealed by weeks under the stars.
It isn't important that the story be my story.

Other people are always stealing strangers' lives to make themselves into writers. What's important is that fans of horror enjoy reading my story while snug in their beds.

I'm waiting like someone who doesn't know what awaits her.

No, I'm waiting like someone who will live to tell of it, someone free and trembling between fort and sea, while the Englishman takes photos of fishing skiffs and the grandchildren of those who weren't enslaved sell cans of warm Coca-Cola and postcards of the Middle Passage.

Real life won't let me play all the parts I rehearsed for myself while idling along with the tour guide. In the end, I'll leave Elmina Castle through the same passageway over which they wrote *The Door of No Return*, and I'll play the part of a tourist, soon to cross the sea of her own free will, into the New World.

AS IF THE WORLD WERE
MISSING A BLUE WINDOW

Nothing will happen but nothing will stay the same. Before the end of the year, you'll cross the sea and I'll cross the ocean to meet in a city located at a seemly distance from each of our homes. You'll translate some stories about sorceresses and demons to buy the ticket, I'll invent a transparent lie to leave Christmas dinner warm on the table and not miss my plane.

My body reposes atop the clouds. I'll remember each one on my way to you, since it won't be there for the return flight. The rain that rises now as steam from the waters will become water again. It's not by accident that I spend my flight reading *The Museum of Innocence*. This won't make Pamuk happy, though it might make the museum's founder feel less melancholy.

All just to be here in a carpet store, about to buy the one full of defects for our shared room. We don't lie to the old rug merchant: We're both from Egypt and despite geography, despite the separate paths our lives have taken, we're here, together.

*

We exchange gifts that couldn't be sent by mail: a bracelet for a ring, *The Tobacco Keeper* for *The World Doesn't End*. We drill a peephole in the wall that separates us.

—You sleep a lot, sweetie, and never in my life have I seen someone drink coffee with Coca-Cola.

—You have an intimate relationship with your toothbrush, my love, and I've never met someone who had such raspy lungs that she forgets to breathe when she laughs.

—You went back to Egypt at the right time.

—You left Egypt at the right time.

You buy my son a piece of agate, I buy your mother a kohl jar. On the way home, each of us thinks, *I wonder what the right time is?*

*

Each of us goes home. Kisses on the neck, scratch marks on the back. Scents in the skin, pain beneath.

That's how we planned a crime that would hurt no one but ourselves. You have manuscripts to edit, while I go back to roost atop my silence. The streets of Cairo are still crowded—just open the window. But I can't believe the mountains are where they used to be. For me, the closest place at a safe distance from this desolation is death.

*

Impossible for me to see you in a city with no walls: here the winds moan beyond the city gates, unable to enter. A walled city—both of us need a prison to notice the birds flying above it. It depressed me to think they were seagulls. How could such wings belong to egg thieves? It depressed you to think they were seagulls. How could these symbolic creatures, the subjects of poets' songs, feed on garbage?

*

You search for love, then don't know what to do with it. Hand clutches hand, then fears what it holds will never let go. The ear gets used to one voice, which quickly becomes insufferable. It's like I'm peering into the darkness of the womb, looking for the lucky little egg, clinging like her to the side of the wall, waiting together for the moment of maturity and freedom, warmth and fulfillment, embodiment and creation, unsure whether life truly needs another child or not.

Love: again. Magnificent delusion we bring to life and then try to control.

*

I'm intoxicated, you're infatuated   so who will take us home?

An open question, like a wound—a question we call *existential*. But it's the taxi driver who will take us back to the hotel. And so we disappoint the ancient poet with our facile answers.

*

Like a little hole dug by settlers to torture local rebels, as terrifying as a deep well . . . The will to crime crumbles at the thought of punishment; victims' souls circle the dim light. Bats crash against the walls of memory. Having escaped the bottle, the jinn don't know what to do.

He and I
I'll say to myself someday:
We were there as hostages
to a desire that felt like despair.
I put my emigration and his estrangement
on the golden scales
and suddenly we were rich.
Each of us tried to overpower the other,
looking for a freedom we had no reason to expect.
We were wise enough to renounce our self-absorption
    and go back
to our roles as upstanding citizens in a modern society,
leaving our two beautiful bodies in that little hole.
It couldn't possibly have been a hotel room.

*

Dawn is when the heart gets pulled in two directions. The sun hasn't yet opened her eyes, the moon hasn't yet gone to bed . . .

No dew gathers on the argan tree, which survives even the longest droughts.

I feel the desire to pray. I don't know whom to address.

With his hand
by my hair
a man pulled me up
when I was drowning after walking
on water
an ark made of gold split in two
with a forest in the middle
and a sun that was like the sun
a cinerous wave of velvet but no ashes
a museum for everything extinct
and still deeper down
tiny fish swam into my lungs
and by my hair
with his hand
a man pulled me up until I twisted in the wind
time streamed past
and the mountains wavered between flames and light
all this happened before I returned to the shore
my dress torn
feeling the sand's firmness
and now that I'm here

I'm not frightened of the sea
for the closed book of desire
is open
with a bookmark on one of its pages.

FROM THE WINDOW

You recognize the one who was broken, the one whose spine they managed to straighten, whose neck they managed to stick back on his shoulders.

From where you stand, drinking coffee and watching the passersby, you can guess at the line of the vein they threaded from his wrist to his heart, and you can see the glint of the pins they imported for surgery.

You notice how carefully he takes his steps as he walks slowly in a straight line, never turning around so you might see his eyes. This one's sealed tight.

It'll be easier with one who was blown apart. The one who was blown apart often turns around, as though looking for a part that's still missing. He sometimes smiles sweetly, because they've patched him together with gum, or frowns bitterly, because he's used too much glue to plug the space between two limbs.

I don't think you can make out from the window the ones who were torn to shreds. There's really nothing to identify them!

Or else, each of them looks exactly like himself—canceled stamps, unfixed from their envelopes, which ended up in some philatelist's album.

THE IDEA OF HOME

I sold my earrings at the gold store to buy a silver ring in the market. I swapped that for old ink and a black notebook. This was before I forgot my pages on the seat of a train that was supposed to take me home. Whenever I arrived in a city, I felt my home was in a different one.

Olga says, without my having told her any of this, "Your home is never really home until you sell it. Then you discover all the things you could do with the garden and the large rooms—like you're seeing it through the eyes of a broker. You stored all your nightmares in the attic, now you have to pack them in a suitcase or two." Olga falls silent, then suddenly smiles, a monarch among her subjects, there in the kitchen between her coffee machine and a window with a view of flowers.

Olga's husband wasn't there to witness this queenly speech. Maybe that's why he still thinks the house will be a loyal friend even when he loses his sight—a house whose foundations will hold steady, whose stairs will mercifully protect him from falls in the dark.

I'm digging around for a key that always gets lost in the bottom of my handbag, here where neither Olga nor her husband can see me, training myself in reality so I can give up the idea of home.

Every time you go back home with the dirt of the world under your nails, you stuff everything you could carry with you into its closets. But you refuse to define home as the resting place of junk, as a place where these dead things were once confused with hope. Let home be that place where you never notice the bad lighting, let it be a wall whose cracks keep growing until one day you take them for doors.

ACKNOWLEDGMENTS

Our thanks to the editors of the following publications, where these poems, sometimes in different form, first appeared: *The Arkansas International*, *Home: New Arabic Poems* (Two Lines Press), *The Nation*, *The New Republic*, *The New York Review of Books*, *The Paris Review*, *Poetry London*, *The Threepenny Review*, *Virginia Quarterly Review*, and *The Yale Review*.

The translator is also grateful to the National Endowment for the Arts, whose support was crucial to the completion of this book.